Ancient
Egyptian
Warfare

By Phyllis G. Jestice

Please visit our Web site at www.garethstevens.com
For a free color catalog describing Gareth Stevens Publishing's
list of high-quality books call 1-800-542-2595 (USA)
or 1-800-387-3187 (Canada).

Library of Congress Cataloging-in-Publication Data

Jestice, Phyllis G.
    Ancient Egyptian Warfare / by Phyllis G. Jestice.
        p. cm. — (Ancient Warfare)
    Includes bibliographical references and index.
    ISBN-10: 1-4339-1971-0   (lib. bdg.)
    ISBN-13: 978-1-4339-1971-8   (lib. bdg.)
    1. Military art and science—Egypt-History—To 500—Juvenile literature.
    2. Egypt—History, Military—Juvenile literature.   3. Military art and science—History—To 500—
Juvenile literature.   4. Military history, Ancient—Juvenile literature.   I. Title.
    U31.J47   2009
    355.020932—DC22   2009006189

This North American edition first published in 2010 by
GS Learning Library
1 Reader's Digest Road
Pleasantville, NY 10570-7000 USA

Copyright © 2010 by Amber Books, Ltd.
Produced by Amber Books Ltd., Bradley's Close
74–77 White Lion Street
London N1 9PF, U.K.

Amber Project Editor: James Bennett
Amber Designer: Joe Conneally

Gareth Stevens Executive Managing Editor: Lisa M. Herrington
Gareth Stevens Editor: Joann Jovinelly
Gareth Stevens Senior Designer: Keith Plechaty

Interior Images
All illustrations © Amber Books, Ltd., except:
AKG Images: 23 (Andrea Jemolo), 28 (Erich Lessing); Art Archive: 3 (Gianni Dagli Orti), 6, 7 (Gianni Dagli Orti/Egyptian
Museum, Cairo), 9 (Alfredo Dagli Orti/Egyptian Museum, Cairo), 11 (Gianni Dagli Orti/Egyptian Museum, Cairo), 16
(Gianni Dagli Orti/Egyptian Museum, Turin), 19b (Gianni Dagli Orti/Musée du Louvre Paris), 22 (Gianni Dagli Orti/Luxor
Museum, Egypt), 25 (Gianni Dagli Orti/Archaeological Museum, Istanbul), 27 (Gianni Dagli Orti);
Bridgeman Art Library: 18 (Egyptian National Museum, Cairo); Corbis: 1 (Araldo de Luca), 8 (Roger Wood), 13 (Alfredo
Dagli Orti/Art Archive), 20 (Carl & Ann Purcell), 21 (Araldo de Luca), 24 (Sandro Vannini); Public Domain: 26

Cover Images
Front Cover: Left, painted relief of Ramses II (Photos.com); top right, Ramses II at the Battle of Kadesh (G. Dagli Orti/De
Agostini Picture Library); Center right, ancient Egyptian water-clock (De Agostini Picture Library); Bottom right, gold
dagger and sheath from the Tutankhamun treasure (Egyptian National Museum/Bridgeman Art Library)
Back Cover: Center, parchment (James Steidl/Dreamstime); right, Old Kingdom archer (Amber Books)

Printed in the United States of America

1 2 3 4 5 6 7 8 9 13 12 11 10 09

Contents

CHAPTER 1

Foot Soldiers

In about 3150 B.C., in northeastern Africa, a king named Narmer united ancient Egypt. He defeated a ruler from the north and formed a single kingdom out of Upper Egypt in the Nile River valley and Lower Egypt in the Nile **Delta**. The Nile River provided ancient Egyptians with water to grow crops and feed cattle, and mud to build bricks for shelters. After the kingdom was united, ancient Egyptian **civilization** thrived. Narmer had built a capital city, Memphis, on the Nile. Kings became known as **pharaohs**. Imhotep, an architect and physician, designed the first **pyramid**. That became known as the step pyramid at Saqqara.

The ancient Egyptians were a religious culture. They worshipped more than 200 gods. Temples were built to practice religious ceremonies, and priests and

▶ **FOOT SOLDIERS**
Egyptian foot soldiers from the Old Kingdom used large shields to defend themselves from their enemies' weapons.

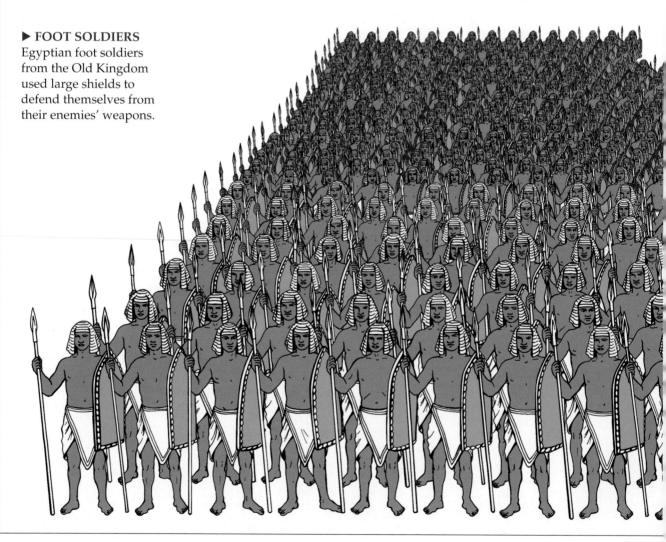

priestesses performed daily rituals honoring Egyptian gods.

The Egyptian civilization was also long lasting. Historians divide its 3,000-year existence into periods. Those periods include the Old Kingdom (2886–2151 B.C.), the Middle Kingdom (2055–1650 B.C.), and the New Kingdom (1550–1069 B.C.). The ancient Egyptian civilization ended in 30 B.C. with the death of Cleopatra, its last ruler.

Early Years

Early Egypt was peaceful. For years after Narmer's victory, fighting between Egyptians was rare. Egypt's natural geography helped protect it from outside invaders. There was harsh desert to the west of Egypt, and the Red Sea to its east. To the north was the Mediterranean Sea. Rough territory lay between Egypt and Palestine in the northeast.

Egypt's enemies lived to its south, in Nubia, to its west, in Libya, and to its east, in Arabia. Because fighting was rare, Egyptian warfare improved slowly. Early Egyptians kept armies, but soldiers used only simple weapons such as spears, daggers, and throwing sticks. Those were small curved weapons made from wood, which were also used for hunting.

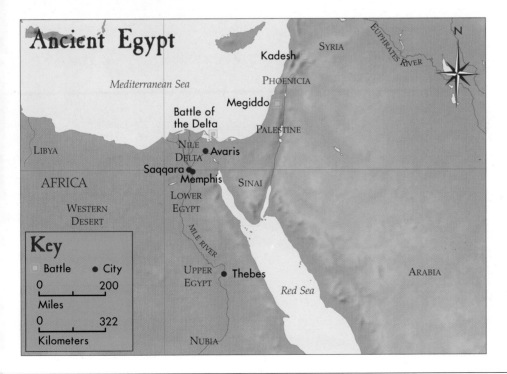

◄ A PROTECTED LAND
This map shows how well Egypt was protected from its enemies by its natural geography. It was very difficult to travel in the Western Desert. The Sinai is still some of the roughest country in the world.

Invasions into Egypt by neighboring people took place during the Old Kingdom, but fighting was rare and disorganized. At that time the efforts of most Egyptian men were focused on farming or building pyramids and tombs.

It wasn't until about 1650 B.C., when the Hyksos invaded northern Egypt, that the Egyptians needed better tactics and weapons. At that time, Egypt did not have a permanent army. Foot soldiers were gathered as needed. During the Middle Kingdom, the governor of

each **nome**, or province, was responsible for grouping soldiers—often under orders from the king. Nobles and rich members of society served as officers. Villagers, farmers, and other workers were forced to fight. They had no choice. **Scribes** traveled to each settlement

and made lists of the strongest, healthiest men. Those men became soldiers. Foreign soldiers such as Nubians, Libyans, and **Phoenicians** were also used as **mercenaries**, or hired soldiers.

At first, soldiers fought very little. They mostly guarded forts and defended the southern border with Nubia. Soldiers kept the Nubians at bay, and once in a while fighting edged north toward Palestine.

The First Army

The first Egyptian army was divided into archers and foot soldiers. Archers used simple curved bows and arrows and fought in pairs. On the battlefield, each archer stood behind a large shield held by his partner. The archers and soldiers needed shields to protect them. They did not have body armor or helmets. Foot soldiers fought with spears, **maces**, or hand axes with wide

◀ PROTECTION IN THE AFTERLIFE
In ancient Egypt, the dead were buried with everything they thought they would need in the afterlife. That included everything from food and drink to models of soldiers. These model Nubian soldiers were found in a New Kingdom tomb.

They settled in the region, increasing in number as the years passed. Eventually they conquered northern Egypt. The Hyksos ruled the region as kings for 200 years. The Egyptians used that time to improve their weapons and fighting skills. They also learned to make and use horse-drawn chariots.

In the improved Egyptian army, men served their entire lives as soldiers. Being a soldier became an important and respected job. Soldiers could improve their status in society. High-ranking soldiers were rewarded with land, gold, and slaves. Scribes and men from lower ranks could work their way up to higher positions if they were educated.

▲ DEFENSE OF THE SOUTH
The Egyptians built fortresses to defend their southern border from the Nubians. This fort at Buhen was home to about 1,000 soldiers. Its ruins stand on the banks of the Nile River.

blades. During battle, archers formed lines on either side of the commander. They fired their arrows toward the enemy. The foot soldiers followed behind, killing any enemies they found.

Young men served as many as six years in the army, often in harsh conditions. Their training was brutal. Food and water were limited. Soldiers had to be fit. They wrestled to improve their strength.

The Hyksos

Egyptian warfare changed after the Hyksos invaded northern Egypt in about 1650 B.C. The Hyksos first arrived in the Nile Delta.

DID YOU KNOW?

It was during the New Kingdom that the Egyptians began calling their king pharaoh. The word means "great house" or "palace." Pharaohs headed the government, kept law and order, and served as military leaders.

An Army of Conquest

At the heart of Egypt's improved army were chariot fighters. Horse-drawn chariots were very expensive, though, so most of the army fought on foot. As time passed, Egyptian soldiers fought enemies who used protective body armor. Older Egyptian maces and slashing axes could not pierce armor, so soldiers began using axes with sharp, narrower heads that could. Egyptian soldiers also adopted body armor made of **bronze**. Best of all, soldiers began using **composite bows**, which could fire arrows much farther than simple bows.

Typical battles started with archers. They shot arrows at enemy arms and legs—the only areas not covered with armor. Chariots came in from the sides, followed by foot soldiers. Those soldiers killed people the chariot fighters had only wounded. Finally, full teams of soldiers rushed forward to kill any enemies who had not run away.

▼ **FIGHTING PHARAOH**
Pharaoh Ramses II (1303–1213 B.C.) wanted his tomb to show everyone that he was a powerful and victorious ruler. This wall painting from his tomb shows him preparing to kill a group of captured enemies from Syria, Nubia, and Libya.

CHAPTER 2

Fighting with Horses

Before the Hyksos invasion, the Egyptians fought only on foot. Horses arrived in Egypt in about 2100 B.C., between the Old and Middle Kingdoms. When the Hyksos conquered northern Egypt, they used horses and chariots. That gave them a powerful advantage over the Egyptians. For about 500 years, armies that used chariots defeated armies that did not. The Egyptians had a few mounted soldiers called **scouts**. Their horses were too small to be used as **cavalry**. Once Egyptians included chariots in their army, they quickly became leaders in warfare.

Using war chariots was costly. That was because the expense of keeping a team of horses to pull them was high. Chariots also had to be repaired. People were needed to

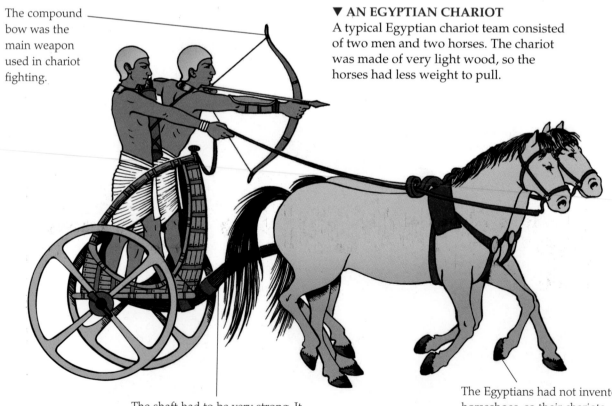

The compound bow was the main weapon used in chariot fighting.

▼ AN EGYPTIAN CHARIOT
A typical Egyptian chariot team consisted of two men and two horses. The chariot was made of very light wood, so the horses had less weight to pull.

The shaft had to be very strong. It was made from imported wood.

The Egyptians had not invented horseshoes, so their chariots could not ride on rough ground.

DID YOU KNOW?

When the tomb of Egyptian King Tutankhamun ("King Tut") was explored, archaeologists found four dismantled chariots for the king to use in the afterlife.

maintain them. Because few Egyptians could afford them, most chariot fighters were from the wealthiest classes of Egyptian society. Chariot fighters were honored and respected. Egyptian pharaohs who took part in fighting always rode into battle on chariots.

A Chariot Force

Within a century of the Hyksos invasion, chariot fighters became the center of the Egyptian army. Chariot fighters worked as a team. Each chariot had two horses joined together by hardware that pulled the vehicle. One man either shot arrows or threw **javelins**. The other drove the chariot, holding a large shield to protect his partner and himself.

The Egyptians had not only adopted the use of the chariot, they improved it. Egyptian chariots were lighter, faster, and more flexible than earlier designs. They could also dart in and out of spaces with ease. An Egyptian chariot was about 3 feet (1 meter) wide. It

▼ TUTANKHAMUN'S CHARIOT

This is an example of a chariot that was found in Tutankhamun's tomb. Egyptian chariots look simple, but were very difficult to make. They had to be very light, but sturdy enough to survive a battle.

The horses were attached with a simple yoke around their necks. If there was too much weight they could choke.

A chariot was so light that one man could carry it.

Chariots originally had solid wheels. The invention of open wheels with spokes made chariots much lighter.

had two wheels and a floor made of woven animal skin, and it was light enough for one man to carry on his back. Chariots had to be as lightweight as possible because of the way the horses were harnessed. Nobody had invented the horse collar yet, so the soldiers harnessed horses the way they would oxen. They placed a thin wooden bar under the horse's neck. If the horses had to pull too hard because the chariot was heavy, they could choke on the **yoke**.

Egyptian chariots were not designed to crash into the enemy, but to move quickly.

Chariot fighters rode as close as possible to enemy soldiers so they could reach out and use their weapons. They then rode away before enemy soldiers could get close enough to kill them. Sometimes **Hittite** (HIT-tight) soldiers on chariots rode close enough to the enemy to stab them with long spears. Egyptians did not stab enemy soldiers. They preferred to kill with arrows, firing their weapons from chariots as they sped along.

By 1500 B.C., chariot teams made up nearly half of some Egyptian armies.

When the Egyptian king Thutmose III (Thut-MOSE-uh) won the battle of Megiddo in 1458 B.C., he boasted that he had captured 924 enemy chariots. Chariots were important in Egyptian warfare until about 1000 B.C., when cavalry replaced many of them.

▼ WARRIOR KING
Thutmose III (1479–1425 B.C.) was one of the greatest generals of Egyptian history. He fought several wars with the kings of Palestine, including his great victory at Megiddo.

2 **A Surprise Attack**
Foot soldiers from the prince of Kadesh's army guarded another entrance to the valley. The group was shocked when the Egyptian soldiers attacked without warning.

3 **Late and Disorganized**
Prince Kadesh rushed his troops to stop the Egyptians, but had too little time to put them in order before the Egyptian troops attacked.

5 **Fleeing in Panic**
The army of Kadesh fled. The Egyptian chariots killed many enemy soldiers as they ran away.

Key

Prince of Kadesh's Army

Egyptian Army

1 Ready and Waiting

Thutmose arranged the Egyptian troops for battle before enemy troops arrived. Chariots were positioned in front and foot soldiers followed behind.

4 Terrifying Chariot Charge

Egyptian chariots charged down the hill at the enemy, shooting arrows and causing panic, with foot soldiers following behind.

The Battle of Megiddo
1458 B.C.

The battle of Megiddo is the oldest battle in history for which historians have details. It was fought in 1458 B.C., the first year that Thutmose III ruled Egypt. The account, carved on the wall of a temple, shows Thutmose III was a great leader.

The prince of Kadesh (Ka-DESH), a city-state in Syria, wanted to take control of the city of Megiddo in Palestine. Megiddo was important to Egypt, so Thutmose III marched north to save it. He rushed his men through the hard, dry land and reached Megiddo before the enemy expected him. His advisers had told him to take an easier road, but Thutmose was bold. He took his men through a narrow pass to save time and arranged them for battle before the enemy arrived. The Egyptian chariots swept around the enemy, attacking from the sides and back. Finally, the enemy forces were overcome. Kadesh's army fled to the city, leaving their chariots and armor behind.

CHAPTER 3

Weapons and Armor

The first Egyptian weapons were spears, clubs, or maces. A mace is a club with a heavy head made of stone or metal. Maces were especially dangerous to enemies not wearing helmets. Egyptians also used cutting axes. Those had wide, flat edges that could slash the enemy. But axes could not get through armor, and they sometimes broke during battle.

The Egyptians needed to improve their weapons.

Early Egyptian bows and arrows were also simple. The bow was a long piece of springy wood, bent into a curve with string. Arrows were made of light reeds from the Nile, with stone tips attached. Shields for both archers and foot soldiers were made of animal skin stretched on wooden frames.

DID YOU KNOW?

Early Egyptians broke into enemy forts by poking at the mud-brick walls with poles. They even chopped the bricks with axes, to make parts of the walls tumble.

▶ ANCIENT MACES

Egyptian war maces like these were used from around 4000 B.C. The stone heads have holes drilled into them so they stay attached to the wooden shafts. The mace on the right has a disc shape. The sharp edge made the disc mace a fearsome weapon against an enemy who was not wearing a helmet.

Improvements

The Egyptians' use of simple weaponry changed after the Hyksos invasion of northern Egypt. The Hyksos were used to fighting in western Asia, near Palestine and Syria. Those kingdoms and tribes fought each other all the time. Compared to the Egyptians, who fought rarely, the people of Asia were always improving their weapons. The Hyksos wore protective

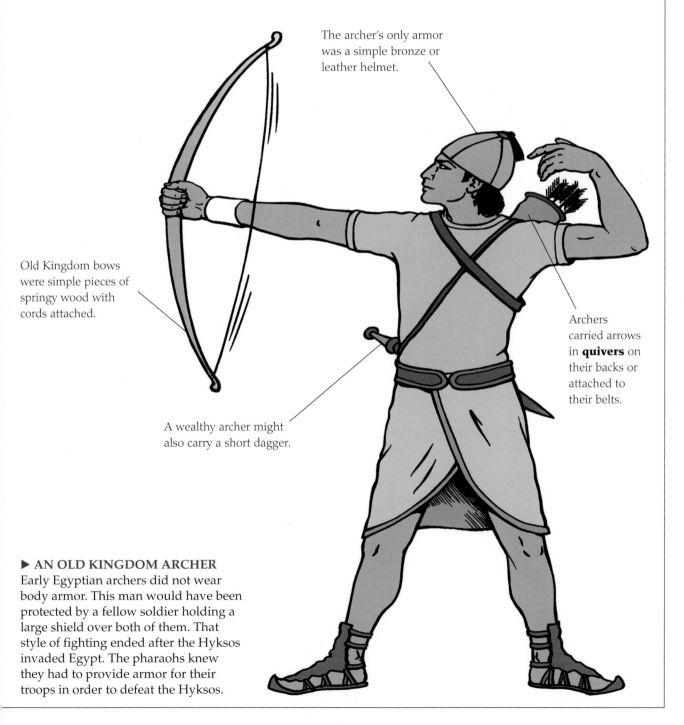

The archer's only armor was a simple bronze or leather helmet.

Old Kingdom bows were simple pieces of springy wood with cords attached.

Archers carried arrows in **quivers** on their backs or attached to their belts.

A wealthy archer might also carry a short dagger.

▶ **AN OLD KINGDOM ARCHER**
Early Egyptian archers did not wear body armor. This man would have been protected by a fellow soldier holding a large shield over both of them. That style of fighting ended after the Hyksos invaded Egypt. The pharaohs knew they had to provide armor for their troops in order to defeat the Hyksos.

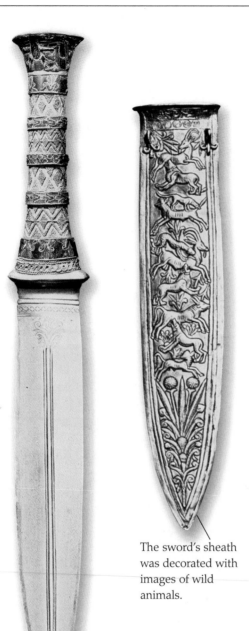

The sword's sheath was decorated with images of wild animals.

The blade was made from hardened gold.

▲ KING TUT'S DAGGER

This gold dagger and its **sheath** were found in Tutankhamun's tomb. An iron dagger was also discovered there. It is one of the earliest iron weapons ever found.

helmets and body armor made of bronze and leather. They also had long daggers and axes with narrow cutting blades, which could pierce armor. Bronze weapons were new to the Egyptians.

Composite bows were among the most important weapons the Hyksos brought to Egypt. Composite bows were stronger and more powerful than simple Egyptian bows. They were made of layers of horn and animal tendon glued together around wooden cores. It took great strength to shoot a composite bow, but the results were worth the effort. A composite bow could shoot arrows about 350 yards (320 meters). In fact, until the early 1800s, a composite bow was deadlier than a modern rifle because it could shoot farther and faster than a gun could shoot a bullet.

Bronze Age Weapons

Over time, Egyptians needed stronger weapons made of harder metals. Among those weapons was the **sickle sword**. That was a long-handled axe cast in one piece of bronze, so it never fell apart. Sickle swords gave the Egyptians a real edge

DID YOU KNOW?

The ancient Egyptians smeared battle wounds with wild honey, which protected them from germs.

against the Nubians, an ongoing enemy. (Egyptians had copper, but they were forced to import all of the tin required to make bronze, which is **forged** from a mixture of tin and copper.)

The Egyptians did not use sickle swords for long. They needed even heavier weapons, such as bronze piercing axes and long daggers to get through their enemies' body armor. In addition, Egyptians began using reed arrows with bronze tips. The Egyptians also made body armor from linked pieces of bronze.

A handle was attached to the sickle sword with rivets.

▶ **THREE SICKLE SWORDS**
The sickle sword was actually a type of improved axe, cast in one piece of bronze. Sickleswords were better than earlier axes because they never fell apart during battle.

The sharp edge of a sickle sword was shaped like a traditional axe blade.

◀ **SIMPLE WAR AXE**
Egyptian war axes were usually simple bronze blades tied onto wooden handles.

▼ **CAST IN BRONZE**
This is a more advanced axe. Later axes like this one were cast as one piece of bronze.

CHAPTER 4

Great Leaders

The Ancient Egyptians believed their devotion and respect for the gods would keep them safe. They also believed that the ruling pharaoh was a living god. Each pharaoh was considered the son of Amun, the greatest and most powerful of all the Egyptian gods. That meant that the pharaoh was in charge of maintaining order on Earth. He led and directed the troops. He received advice from his captains, but made decisions alone. This was especially true during the New Kingdom, the time of Egypt's great warrior-kings. Ahmose, Thutmose III, Ramses II, and Ramses III were heroes because of their military successes.

▶ **RAMSES II**
Ramses II (1303–1213 B.C.) was one of the greatest warrior kings of Egypt. He had built enormous statues of himself to boast of his victories.

HISTORY OF EGYPTIAN WARFARE

OLD KINGDOM	MIDDLE KINGDOM			
3000 B.C.	2000 B.C.	1650 B.C.	1600 B.C.	1550 B.C.
3150 Narmer unites Egypt.		**1650** Hyksos invade Egypt.		**1554–1534** Kamose and Ahmose I defeat the Hyksos.

► **ROYAL SPHINX**

Egyptian kings were not modest. They filled Egypt with paintings and statues of themselves. This sphinx—a statue of a lion with a human head—has the features of Ahmose I (1560–1525 B.C.) who drove the Hyksos from Egypt.

The Reconquest

During the New Kingdom, the Egyptians reclaimed northern Egypt from the Hyksos. Lower Egypt in the north and Upper Egypt in the south were again united. Egypt entered its golden age.

Defeating a strong enemy like the Hyksos changed the way Egyptians viewed the world. After, Egyptian kings

DID YOU KNOW?

The goddess of destruction and war in Egypt was Sekhmet, the lioness. Sekhmet could be vengeful, but she also had the job of protecting the king.

NEW KINGDOM

1500 B.C.	1450 B.C.	1400 B.C.	1350 B.C.	1300 B.C.	1250 B.C.	1200 B.C.	1150 B.C.
1506–1493	**1479–1425** Thutmose III			**1333–1324** **1285** Battle of Kadesh		**1175** Battle of the Delta	
Thutmose I	**1458** Battle of Megiddo			Tutankhamun	**1279–1213** Ramses II	**1186–1155** Ramses III	

decided that all the people of the **Near East** were their enemies. During the New Kingdom period, the Egyptians built a stronger army and started a series of wars. Their goal was to conquer Palestine and beyond, fighting the Hittites and others for control of Syria. The Egyptians also conquered Nubia to the south.

Beginning in 1600 B.C., Sekenenre, the king of Thebes (THEE-bz), who ruled over Upper Egypt in the south, started a long war. He wanted to take northern Egypt back from the Hyksos. The fight started when Sekenenre led raids against the Hyksos. The Theban king was killed in battle by repeated axe blows to the head. Historians know this from examining his **mummy**.

Sekenenre's young sons Kamose (Kah-MOSE-uh) and Ahmose (Ah-MOSE-uh)

This tablet is written in **hieroglyphs**, a form of picture writing where each figure or group of figures stands for a sound or a whole word.

◄ **A RECORD OF KAMOSE'S VICTORY**
When Kamose won his first great battle against the Hyksos, he created this large stone tablet, telling everyone that he was the true king of all Egypt.

Although it looks like this axe head is bound to the handle, it is only a decoration. This weapon was cast from one piece of bronze.

This axe is decorated with pictures of several Egyptian gods, as well as lotus and **papyrus** plants, symbols of ancient Egypt.

▼ THE AXE OF AHMOSE I
This axe belonged to Ahmose I, who drove the Hyksos out of Egypt. He may have used this axe in battle, more than 3,500 years ago.

In Their Own Words

"What power can I claim to have, when I am stuck between an Asiatic and a Nubian? Each of them has a piece of Egypt too, and shares the land with me. My aim is to liberate Egypt...."

—Kamose, after learning that the Hyksos and Nubian kings wanted to capture Egypt, 1560 B.C.

were outraged by their father's murder. They wanted to avenge his death by reclaiming Egypt for the Egyptians. Not all Egyptians wanted to fight, however. Many were tolerant of Hyksos leadership. The Egyptians still had the best crops, and their animals had plenty to eat.

But the Egyptians' attitudes soon changed. Egyptian spies working for Kamose captured a Hyksos messenger in the desert. He was carrying a letter from the Hyksos king to the king of Nubia, Egypt's other enemy to the south. The letter was an invitation to the Nubian king to have his armies join his fight to capture the rest of Egypt. It said, *"Come north, there is no need to worry, Kamose is busy with me here. We'll divide the towns of Egypt between us and Nubia will rejoice."*

Kamose knew it was time to act. He had his soldiers moved down the Nile by ship, and they took the Hyksos towns one by one. The last battle took place in the city of Avaris, the Hyksos capital. Ahmose **besieged** the city for seven months before he broke in to kill his enemies. The Hyksos were nearly defeated when Kamose suddenly died. Kamose's younger brother Ahmose was left to lead Egypt's troops. After another decade of fighting, Egypt was finally reunited. The Hyksos occupation was over. Ahmose was worshipped as a god.

DID YOU KNOW?
It was important for Egyptian rulers to look like warriors in their statues and paintings. Even Queen Hatshepsut was shown in art as a male warrior, complete with a beard.

Thutmose III, Warrior King

After defeating the Hyksos, the Egyptians looked northeast, outside Egypt's borders. Thutmose I, who became king in 1493 B.C., had once tried to take an army to Palestine. But the troops reached only as far as the Euphrates River in Syria. The greatest warrior-king was his grandson, Thutmose III. Usually, Egyptian kings spent most of their time governing. But Thutmose III became king as a child, and his stepmother—the **regent** queen Hatshepsut (Hat-SHEP-sut)—was not willing to give him the throne when he grew up. As a young man, Thutmose III had plenty of time for war. He led 17 military **campaigns**, mostly to Palestine, and won them all.

◄ KING THUTMOSE III
In this wall painting, Thutmose wears the blue war helmet of an Egyptian king.

When the Egyptians made peace with an enemy, they had a treaty carved in stone and set in a public place. That way, everyone could know if either leader broke his agreement. This is the peace treaty created after the battle of Kadesh in 1285 B.C.

Ramses II at Kadesh

Egypt had other great warrior-kings, especially Ramses II (RAM-is-seez). He is known to have reigned for 66 years, longer than any other Egyptian king. Ramses II boasted he won the battle of Kadesh against the Hittites, but the battle actually ended in a ceasefire. Both sides claimed victory. After 15 years, the Egyptians and Hittites made peace and united. They wanted to join forces to fight the Assyrians, a common enemy.

In 1285 B.C., Ramses II led an Egyptian army against the Hittites. Both sides were fighting for control of Palestine, especially Kadesh. Hittite scouts made Ramses think that the Hittite army was far away, but it was actually nearby. While the Egyptians set up camp, the Hittites launched a surprise attack. Ramses said that only his quick thinking saved the Egyptians. He took his chariots forward in a move that held off the enemy until the rest of the Egyptian army could arrive.

CHAPTER 5

War at Sea

Ancient Egypt was a long, thin region stretched over two kingdoms. Those kingdoms were Upper Egypt in the Nile River Valley and Lower Egypt in the Nile Delta. Only a few miles away from the river on either side was desert. Irrigation ditches leading from the Nile divided the land. Armies sailed along the Nile to go from place to place because it was the easiest method of transportation. Life around the Nile was always active. Goods were transported up and down the river by boat. Egyptians fished along the river and gathered its reeds to build rafts and boats as well as a kind of paper called papyrus.

The Royal Navy

Early Egyptians used raft-like sailing boats along the Nile. Those boats moved by wind power and by rowers, but they broke up easily. They could not be sailed in the open sea. The Egyptians used those early vessels to move troops, food, or other supplies along the Nile.

When the Hyksos invaded, naval officers had higher ranks than land officers. Serving

▼ **AN EGYPTIAN RIVER BOAT**
Egyptian sailors used sails when they could, but their ships were also powered by oars. The sail was made from linen cloth or papyrus.

▲ SHIPBUILDERS AT WORK
This ancient Egyptian painting shows men building a trading ship along the Nile River. Egyptian warships were normally larger than trading ships.

as specialists to the army, naval officers helped the Egyptians defeat the Hyksos by moving army units into position. Because the Hyksos also relied on the Nile to transport goods, the Egyptians were able to prevent them from getting food.

By Land and Sea

The navy was always needed to transport soldiers and supplies by sea. When the early Egyptian army fought in Palestine against the Hittites and others, troops built simple sailing boats. The Egyptians had little experience fighting in the open sea, but they used sailing boats to transport troops and goods. Those ships were not strong enough to fight at sea, but they were important to the Egyptians' success. Sailing boats with steering oars could be landed on the coast and unloaded before an enemy knew they

were there. Ships were so important that kings went to great lengths to provide them. During one of his campaigns, Thutmose III ordered that boats be dragged over land by oxen. He wanted to sail them on the Euphrates River.

DID YOU KNOW?

Every year, the Nile flooded its banks. The repeated flooding made the soil rich for farming. The Egyptians called Egypt the "black land," likely named for the fertile soil that provided them with food crops.

The Sea People

The biggest threat to ancient Egypt came from the Mediterranean Sea. Around 1200 B.C., mysterious raiders known as the Sea People attacked many areas in the eastern Mediterranean. Those attackers had new weapons such as swords and javelins that were hard for armies to fight. The Sea People reached Egypt for the second time in 1175 B.C., when Ramses III was king. Finally, the Egyptian sailors had a chance to defeat their mysterious attackers.

The invaders tried to land their ships on the banks of the Nile. In the battle of the Delta, however, Ramses III lined the Nile with archers who shot arrow after arrow at the Sea People. The men in the invading

DID YOU KNOW?

Egypt had so few trees that sometimes the Egyptians made ships by tying together river reeds instead of wood. The Egyptians were forced to import all of their wood from Syria.

▼ **BATTLE OF THE DELTA**
This detail from a wall carving shows how Ramses III defeated the Sea People in around 1175 B.C. The Sea People are shown carrying round shields and wearing helmets with horns.

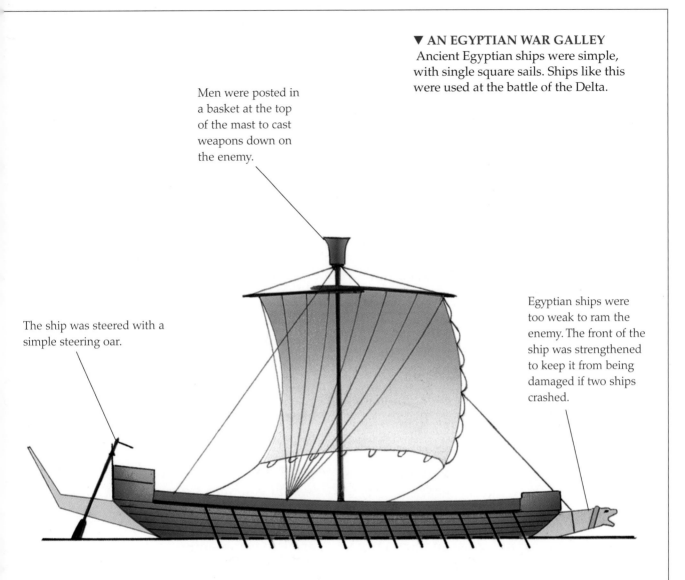

Ancient Egyptian ships were simple, with single square sails. Ships like this were used at the battle of the Delta.

Men were posted in a basket at the top of the mast to cast weapons down on the enemy.

The ship was steered with a simple steering oar.

Egyptian ships were too weak to ram the enemy. The front of the ship was strengthened to keep it from being damaged if two ships crashed.

fleet became disorganized, and the Egyptian navy attacked. The Egyptians threw large hooks at the enemy ships to pull them closer. They then jumped on board and fought in direct, hand-to-hand combat. The Sea People were defeated, and Egypt was saved.

The battle of the Delta was ancient Egypt's last great victory. After, its military became overwhelmed and disorganized. Ramses III fought invaders from Libya, and the growing cost of the army was more than Egypt could afford. In the centuries that followed, Nubians, Assyrians, Babylonians, Persians, Greeks, and Romans conquered Egypt.

The ancient Egyptian civilization was long lasting because of its natural boundaries. Egyptians learned fighting skills from their enemies. They adopted new weapons and armor. They learned to use new technologies, such as the chariot. The Egyptians also built lasting monuments, such as the great pyramids. In the end, ancient Egypt faded away with the death of its last ruler, Cleopatra, in 30 B.C.

Glossary

besieged—surrounded an enemy, a town, a city, or a fortress in order to capture it

bronze—a metal made from tin and copper

campaigns—military operations with specific aims

cavalry—soldiers who fight on horseback

civilization—the people of a particular area and their society, way of life, and culture

composite bows—advanced bows made from wood, animal horn, and sinew

delta—an area at the mouth of a river where the flow divides into several smaller rivers

fleet—a group of ships under one commander

forged—formed by heating and hammering

hieroglyphs—a type of writing where each picture or group of pictures stands for a sound or a whole word

Hittites—an ancient people who lived in parts of present-day Turkey and Syria from around 1750 to 1180 B.C.

javelins—light spears designed to be thrown by hand

maces—weapons with heavy stone or metal head on solid shafts, used in close combat

mercenaries—soldiers who are paid to fight

mummy—a dead body without organs that has been preserved, treated with chemicals, and wrapped in bandages

Near East—the area of southwestern Asia between the Mediterranean Sea and India

nome—a province of ancient Egypt

papyrus—a plant used by the ancient Egyptians to make paper and to build rafts and boats

pharaohs—kings of ancient Egypt

Phoenicians—a seafaring and trading people who lived on the eastern shore of the Mediterranean Sea, in present-day Lebanon and western Syria

pyramid—a building with walls that meet at a point at the top, normally with four sides

quivers—cases that hang from the waist for holding and carrying arrows

regent—an adult who governs on behalf of a child king who is too young to rule

scouts—soldiers who travel in front of an army to gather information

scribes—workers whose job was to write and copy documents

sheath—the protective covering for a dagger or sword

sickle sword—long-handled axe made from one piece of bronze

tutor—a commander in the Egyptian army

yoke—binding around a horse's neck allowing it to pull a chariot or other load

For More Information

Books

Ancient Egypt: A First Look at People of the Nile.
Bruce Strachan (Henry Holt and Co., 2008)

Ancient Egypt. Passport to the Past (series).
Philip Steele (Rosen Publishing, 2009)

The Ancient Egyptians: Dress, Eat, Write, and Play Just Like the Egyptians. Hands-on History (series). Fiona MacDonald
(Crabtree Publishing, 2008)

The Ancient Egyptians. People of the Ancient World (series). Lila Perl (Children's Press, 2005)

Going to War in Ancient Egypt. Armies of the Past (series). Anne Millard (Franklin Watts, 2004)

Life and Times in Ancient Egypt. Life and Times (series). Andrew Charman
(Kingfisher Publishing, 2007)

Ramses the Great. Ancient World Leaders (series). Silvia Anne Sheafer
(Chelsea House, 2008)

The Tomb of King Tutankhamen. Unearthing Ancient Worlds (series). Michael Woods
(Twenty-First Century Books, 2007)

Web Sites

Ancient Egypt
http://www.historyforkids.org/learn/egypt
Read more about ancient Egypt at this web site that features pages about its warfare tactics, government, economy, and daily life.

The British Museum: Ancient Egypt
http://www.ancientegypt.co.uk/menu.html
Take a virtual tour of the ancient Egyptian wing of the British Museum. Click on "Pharaoh" to read the story of a battle told through an ancient wall painting.

Discovering Ancient Egypt by Mark Millmore
http://www.eyelid.co.uk/index.htm
Learn about the pyramids of ancient Egypt, as well as Egyptian pharaohs. This web site is loaded with photographs, maps, and videos.

Mummies of Ancient Egypt
http://www.si.umich.edu/CHICO/mummy
Discover how and why the ancient Egyptians created mummies.

The Quest for Immortality: Treasures of Ancient Egypt
http://www.nga.gov/exhibitions/2002/egypt
Explore life in the ancient world at this web site that is filled with fun facts and pictures, as well as craft projects and other activities.

Index

About the Author

Dr. Phyllis G. Jestice is Assistant Professor of Medieval History at the University of Southern Mississippi. She was previously a Lecturer in Ancient and Medieval History at California State University. She is the author of sections of several other books including *Battles of the Ancient World* and *Battles of the Bible*.